"Brilliantly incisive commentary on our simultaneous human sense of beauty and waste and loss."

Dale Carlson, ALA Notable Book Author

- - - - -

"The French poet and novelist Victor Hugo, wrote, 'The reduction of the universe to the compass of a single being, and the extension of a single being until it reaches God—that is love.' Jennifer A. Payne expands on those words with an unflinching account of our unshakable relationship to the modern world...God, nature, and ourselves."

David W. Berner, Journalist,
National Public Radio Contributor

- - - - -

"The collection of writings and photographs powerfully remind us that our everyday actions effect the environment. Jen Payne's writings underscore our role as stewards and the positive impact we can make on the world around us."

Peter Raymond, Professor, Yale School
of Forestry & Environmental Studies

- - - - -

"*Evidence of Flossing: What We Leave Behind* carries prophetic power in the spaces between its words. It is truth and beauty delivered to us in wide-eyed wonder by a heart passionately in love with nature."

Rita Kowats, Spirituality Without Borders

"In Payne's exquisite introduction to Evidence of Flossing, she provides the purpose of this book: to illustrate, poem by poem, the very fraught relationships which define us, human to human, human to earth and animal, and human to the unifying spirit, which may or may not be her lower case "god." She is sober, admonitory, enraptured and antic by turns, her illustrative photographs always a source of pleasure or irony — often both. This is a most unusual book, richly thoughtful and sorely, sorely needed."

Nancy Fitz-Hugh Meneely,
Author, *Letter from Italy, 1944*

- - - - -

"Evidence of Flossing: What We Leave Behind is, at turns, uplifting, funny, sad, sexy, maddening, silly, educational and, ultimately, a window into the fertile mind of a very thoughtful and creative being. This is what art reads like!"

Greg Sammons, Award-Winning
Graphic Designer/Musician

- - - - -

"It's uncanny how Jen Payne grabs hold of seemingly ordinary strands of life — then surprises us with new meaning. A master at storytelling, Jen brings us to the realization that the stories she shares are actually ours. An engaging, thought provoking and masterful reflection on our collective legacy in this world."

Mary O'Connor, Author/Poet,
Life Is Full of Sweet Spots
and *Dreams of a Wingless Child*

Evidence of Flossing
WHAT WE LEAVE BEHIND

Evidence of Flossing
WHAT WE LEAVE BEHIND
POEMS BY JENNIFER A. PAYNE

Three Chairs
PUBLISHING

BRANFORD, CONNECTICUT

©2017, Jennifer A. Payne, text and photography,
unless otherwise noted.

All rights reserved. No part of this book may be reproduced
or translated in any form or by any means, digital, electronic,
or mechanical, including photocopying, recording, or by any
information storage and retrieval system, without permission in
writing from the publisher, except for the use of brief quotations in
a book review or related article.

Evidence of Flossing: What We Leave Behind
Poems by Jennifer A. Payne
Photography by Jennifer A. Payne, unless otherwise noted
Cover & Book Design by Words by Jen (Branford, CT)
Printed by IngramSpark in the U.S.A.

Library of Congress Control Number: 2017908958

ISBN: 978-0-9905651-1-6

POETRY / Nature
NATURE / Environmental Conservation & Protection
PHOTOGRAPHY / Street Photography

Three Chairs Publishing
P.O. Box 453
Branford, CT 06405

www.3chairspublishing.com

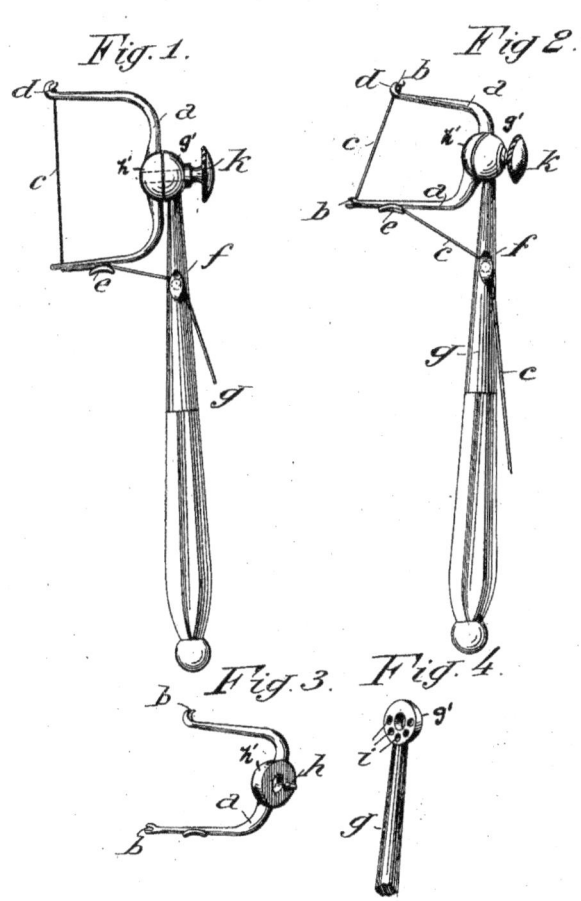

No. 014-0415 - Supply Ponds Nature Preserve, Branford, Connecticut; April 2015

Dedicated to the trailblazers who have taught me to see this world in broader, more beautiful ways: Peter Borgemeister, Lauren Brown, Beth Dock, Bill Horne, Barbara Johnson, Joan & Harry Merrick, Bill Van Wie.

And to Matt Reed, who walks with me in the woods and welcomes both open eyes and an open heart.
xoxo

WITH LOVE & GRATITUDE

It is a true testament of friendship to wait patiently on a street corner while someone takes photos of trash. Even more so to allow time and space for an idea to grow — *There will be photos of dental flossers! And poems! It'll be great!*

It was the magical Ellen Woolf Feichtner who knew the first flosser photos would become a book. Then Judith and Frank Bruder, Dale Carlson, Melissa Cherry, Rhonda Longo, Mary O'Connor, Matt Reed, Mary Anne Siok, Mo Sila, DeLinda Spain, and Martha Link Walsh who lovingly witnessed the transformation from oddball obsession to this: this book. *You are like family, my dear friends; it is a blessing to have you in my life.*

Evidence of Flossing would not be quite as palatable without the wise and thoughtful shepherding of the members of the Guilford Poets Guild: Carol Altieri,

Evelyn Atreya, Gwen Gunn, Julie Harris, Margaret Iacobellis, Karen Johnson, Norman Marshall, Nan Meneely, Jane Muir, Pat O'Brien, Elizabeth Possidente, Jane Ulrich, Ed Walker, and Gordy Whiteman. Their enthusiasm, encouragement, and honest feedback are the glimmering stitches you see throughout this book.

Heartfelt thanks to editors/coaches Dale, Julie, Nan, Mary, and Matt for giving this book (and me) a confident, strong voice.

To Greg Sammons for his good eye, Photoshop wizardry and *atta girls*; to Debbie Hesse for her counsel and encouragement (It was her invitation to participate in the Arts Council of Greater New Haven's exhibit *Where the Whole Universe Dwells* that helped to refine the focus of this book.); to Niki Russell at the Special Collections Department, University of Glasgow Library; Connie Moore, Senior Photo Researcher at NASA Photographic Archival System.

To my nephew Max, who declared flosser #055-0316 "Beautiful!" My life would not be the same without his laugh — *that laugh!* — or his wide-open reminders about wonder, perspective, and seeing things with fresh eyes.

I am forever and always grateful to my Dad, who watches over everything I do with the eyes of a hawk.
I inherited his sense of humor, thank goodness, because humor is an invaluable resource when staring human folly in the face.

```
No. 078-0217 - Life Savers, Pharmacy Parking
Lot, Connecticut; December 2017
```

No. 076-0916 - Old Faithful, Yellowstone National Park, Wyoming; September 2016

TABLE OF CONTENTS

Introduction xiv

About the Flossers xvii

The Grand Intention xix

DAMAGE 1

CONTACT 41

CONNECTION 81

Index of Poems 145

Endnotes 147

About the Author 157

INTRODUCTION

"When we try to pick out anything by itself, we find it hitched to everything else in the Universe."
— John Muir, July 27, 1869[1]

In a dream once, I saw the fabric of the Universe. It was clearly laid out in fine strands of translucent white dots, as if one were standing inside a room full of beaded curtains.

In the first few moments after waking, I understood clearly that everything is connected: how, if I touched one of the rows of white dots, that touch would reverberate along the whole system of dots; if I breathed or sang or wept, that too would make waves along those strands.

My understanding of all of that was as fleeting as my ability to still my mind, as transient as my understanding of god. And yet, the image of those dots has remained for me a divine illustration of how it is.

Everything is connected.

Some of our basic tenets as humans remind us of that: "for every action in nature there is an equal and opposite reaction,"[2] and "as you did it to the least of these my brothers, you did it to me."[3]

Remember the Golden Rule? "Do unto others as you would have them do unto you." What if that applies to everything?

It is not such a foreign concept. We know that everything around us is made up of atoms. That there is no real separation between you, me, this book, my cat. John Muir wrote about it that summer day in 1869: "One fancies a heart like our own must be beating in every crystal and cell."[4] Carl Sagan called it starstuff. "It's an astonishing thing," he said, "we're so tied to the rest of the cosmos."[5]

Evidence of Flossing: What We Leave Behind is a book about starstuff. It's a collection of poems that speak to the common heart that beats in you and in me, in the woods and on the streets, across oceans and around this planet.

Part social commentary, part lament, the poems are, at their heart, love poems to the something greater within all of us. Their investigation of the human condition and its folly — politics, religion, development, technology, consumerism — is juxtaposed to a series of poems about our natural world and the possibility of divine connection. Together, they ask the reader to deeply consider the effects of our actions and how they influence everything else in the Universe.

No. 001-0514 - The flosser that started it all, at the Supply Ponds Nature Preserve in Branford, Connecticut. May 2014.

ABOUT THE FLOSSERS

Scattered throughout this book you will find a series of dental flosser photographs that inspired the title of the book. A take on traditional street photography, these images examine human nature from a different, thought-provoking perspective. Presented as evidence, each flosser photo is captioned with an ID number (series number + discovery date) and location. Part of a collection of more than 100 photographs of discarded flossers found by Jen Payne between 2014 - 2017, they speak to the questions: What will we leave behind? What is our legacy in this vast and wondrous Universe?

What influences how we see the world? What precipitates a change of heart?

The Grand Intention

Perhaps we have always
stood at this precipice —
the tear in our eye
as we consider the right path,
the right action   not yet taken.

In our own lore,
we speak of decisions made
and DAMAGE done;
the casting out of the sinful
for their disrespect
of this gift, this blessing.

With CONTACT, we have
the potential to be
great stewards, caretakers;
in his image, god and creator.

But at what horror,
at what warning,
will we change course?
Choose to see our
innate CONNECTION
to the something greater
and more awesome
than any name   or calling?

At what turning
will we wholly rejoice
the grand intention?

DAMAGE

No. 003-1114 - Car Wash, Connecticut; November 2014

The Times They Are a Changin'

It was, really, a rather ordinary house. Small and sufficient. Big enough for him and for her and children, at some point, I imagine. Red with white trim. A small yard out back.

He would sit on the front stoop and wave if you happened to walk by — a neighborly greeting, no matter your relation. You would often pass her on the sidewalk on your way to the Post Office right next door.

Every year, the arrival of spring was broadcast up and down Park Place by the grand display of two magnificent magnolias. Standing guard at the front walk, they enveloped the home in luscious pink blossoms. Their breezes whispered of age and history and time passing.

Today, a dumpster sits in the yard, overflowing. Sections of the linoleum she paced upon at suppertime, faded wallpaper from the den where he read the paper, the staircase they walked each night, together. And on either side of the front walk, two lifeless stumps broadcasting for all to see — change.

A dentist's office I hear. Bright and shiny. Ordinary.

A Lament for the Parcel at 250 North Main Street

There will be no monument for you.
No quarried pink granite statue,
no sleek wall with carved names,
or plaque at which we leave flowers.

What irony, to leave flowers at *your* grave,
to fingerspell M-A-P-L-E on cold stone,
where hands used to touch warm bark,
feel sweet time seep through veins.

Nothing will fly at half-mast,
not the flag that claims your land,
nor the birds that claimed your branches
as sacred choir loft.

There will be no moment of silence,
no annual tolling of bells
or communal lament for lives lost,
its long list of names retold:

Beech

Birch

Cedar

Cherry

Dogwood

Fir

Hemlock

Hickory

Hornbeam

Laurel

Maple

Oak

Pine

Poplar

Sassafras

Spruce

Tulip

Walnut

As we walk across your grave
for daily purchase and progress,
heads bowed against concrete winds,
no one will weep or remember your songs.

Before & After: 250 North Main Street

Mountain Breeze™

Water

Alcohol Ethoxy Sulfate

Linear Alkylbenzene Sulfonate

Sodium Carbonate

Sodium Chloride

Sodium Polyacrylate

Alcohol Ethoxylate

Fragrance

Fatty Acids

Tetrasodium EDTA

Disodium Diaminostilbene Disulfonate

Methylisothiazolinone

Hexylcinnamaldehyde

D-Limonene

Lilial

Liquitint Blue[6]

Evidence of Flossing: A Random Riff

Would God floss?
Made in his image, we surely do
here, there, and everywhere —
the evidence will bear witness.
But don't bear false witness,
that would be a sin
carved in stone.
Fine line, that sin,
as loose as a filament of floss —
what is right and wrong,
here, there, and everywhere?
Who's to say —
your god or mine?
Rock   Paper   Scissors
My god is bigger than your god!
But by what unit of measure —
metric or imperial?
I suspect imperial
by the long list of *thou shalt nots*.
If such a scale exists, of course.

A scale that measures gods?

What a weighty thought!

As weighty as

considerations of the Universe,

its grand design

a divine creation?

Rock, paper, scissors...

or a boom-town

made from scratch?

Scratch like my Grandmother's

chocolate cake —

a divine creation indeed!

No flosser necessary,

it would melt in your mouth

disappear through pearly whites

— those pearly gates —

pure heaven!

And not a crumb to spare

here, there, or everywhere

because cleanliness is next to godliness after all

and amen to that!

Photo by Kevin Macaranas Domantay

They Know Not What They Do

They speak to

Word of Law,

but what would He

say of the temples

built to commerce,

the worship

of false idols

and profits?

There will be

no salvation

from this —

in our ruins,

only constructs

of fools

and bones of

moneychangers.

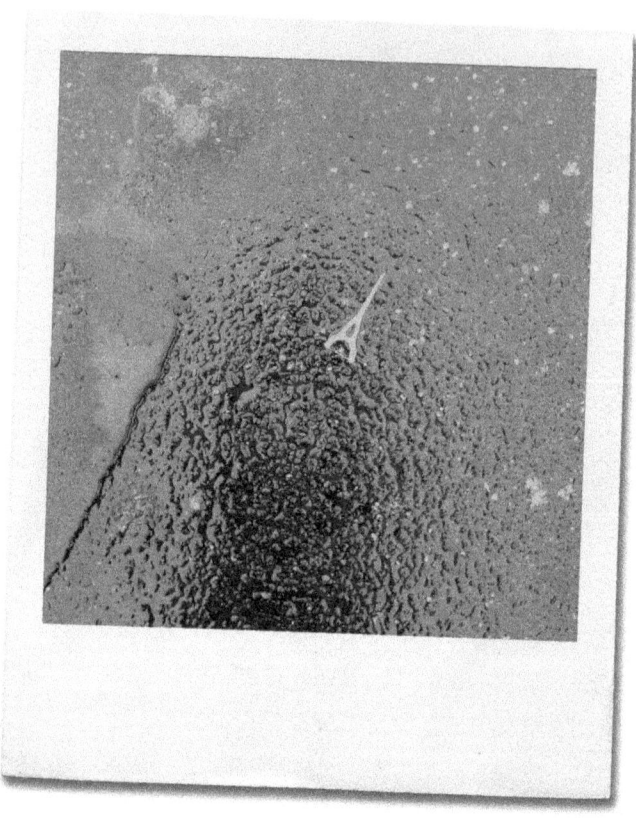

No. 008-1214 - Dollar Store,
Connecticut; December 2014

The Promise of More

Oh good, I just read
we'll have a new store,
I was worried a moment:
where would I buy more?

More trinkets and whatnots,
more must-haves and then,
not one or two thingies,
but eight, nine...no TEN!

Ten more things to purchase,
ten more for display,
ten more for the storage
I rented today!

No. 012-0315 - Sunday on Main Street, Connecticut; March 2015

Sunday at the Dollar Store

She steers her cart
like she's in the parking lot
after 9 a.m. mass at St. Mary's.

Moved by the Spirit she is,
with salvation in sight
there in that votive aisle.

"Why, the Sacred Heart of Jesus
costs only a dollar!" she proclaims,
pushing my cart out of her way.
"And Lord knows that's cheaper
than penance and a tithe."

No. 011-0315 - Print Shop,
Connecticut; March 2015

Mass, Shooting, God, Guns

At the shopping mall

where she bought the onesie

for her sweet little niece,

five people were shot.

She wonders who would do such a thing

— and why?

Just the day before, she walked

by that same cosmetics counter

to the Children's Department,

spotted the rack of pink,

saw the embroidery,

"*Lock up your sons, my daddy has guns.*"

Had it boxed and gift wrapped.

Something is wrong with the world, she thinks,

    then kneels down to pray.

No. 013-0415 - Grocery Store, Connecticut; April 2015

Losing My Religion

The girl who pushed me into walls
sat in front of us at church
on Sundays,
hands folded sweetly,
singing songs of praise
to the god who said
do unto others.

But there was nothing
particularly golden about her,
or my other classmates
who threw stones
and sticks and names
that *did* hurt,
as a matter of fact.

I scheduled an appointment
with the priest
to discuss the contradiction,
but when I got to his house
the door was locked,
so I never went back.

No. 018-0515 - Bank ATM,
Connecticut; May 2015

Sixth Day

The preacher wore a stole of ducks,
stood proud and tall as marsh reed
in a cassock of sport designed
to twist truth and mask intention.

A valiant champion,
pro-faith, pro-God, pro-life,
no doubt preached Genesis
side-by-side with Exodus
in Sunday sermons to the masses.

Two elegant wood ducks,
male and female, mother, father
hung stretched-thin with eyes closed,
in perpetual prayer for the sanctity of life.[7]

Project Limulus

There is an 80 percent survival rate
the intake person tells me
as she notes blood pressure, weight, pulse.

I am a *living fossil* they say,
prehistoric they whisper in the hall,
as old as god.

Soon a technician will pierce my body,
turn me upside down,
drain life force like blue water
from a faucet into glass beakers.

In the waiting room,
shells of selves waste away
like buckets of bait.
The other 20 percent?

All for a good cause of course:
your survival depends on it!

No. NF-005, Horseshoe Crab (Limulus polyphemus) Harvest

Nuisance Species

The over-population they said

    people in the world 7,482,331,668

can lead to excessive noise

    no place on Earth always completely
    free from human sound

and an increased risk of disease

    incidence of common cold: 62 million cases per year

DRC-1339 was the solution

    uremic poisoning and congestion of major organs

a slow, 12 - 72 hour *nonviolent* death

but it sounded violent
    dead birds dropping from trees

and it looked violent
    a galaxy of feathers
    shimmering on the pavement
    iridescent in the afternoon sun

"It's OK," said the man from the USDA, smiling,
"It's not harmful to humans…"

Just the European starlings
in flight, shaped like stars
their cosmic communal dance,
the breathtaking murmurations

communicating

cooperating

connecting[8]

No. 019-0515 - Nature Preserve,
Connecticut; May 2015

No. 017-0515 - New Haven, Connecticut; May 2015

A Righteous Man Regardeth the Life of His Beast

There are some who say
the bear had to be shot.

Why, it tore down a fence,
cussed at a goat and a chicken,
scared a dog or two.

Such crimes against humanity —
just shoot the damn thing!

They'll call it "euthanized" in the papers —
next to the pro-life editorial
and the ad for the candidate who
preaches God from his bully pulpit.

A righteous man regardeth the life of his beast; But the tender mercies of the wicked are cruel. - Proverbs 12:10

COMMON GROUND SERIES

A New York City Schooling

In the shadow of monsters

who will chew us apart

for naught but selfish glory,

I find myself in a school of faces,

caught in a current of humanity

along this city street.

A sea of shapes, sizes, colors,

we're fish-eyed and curious,

moving *en masse*,

fluid in our collaboration—

cooperation, toleration.

The ones with greedy teeth

will never catch that.

No. NF-006, New York City, 2011

False Hope

It's all construct — isn't it?

These gods, demigods and dogmas.

The prayers we offer up now

no more or less real

than any kingdom before —

its princes and emperors

demanding worship

then, now, tomorrow.

How silly this faithful following.

How foolish to dance in these robes,

to sing praises and promises.

In the end, there will be silence,

naked but the peat

and roots that thread ribs.

How futile words in the shadow of that.

Grocery Store: November 2016

We cross paths on common ground,

the one who taught me about god in lowercase,

about the violence of separation, that security is an illusion.

We embrace   kiss cheeks   exhale

and for a brief moment heal our fear,

right the heinous vote of a people divided.

I am not yet fit for human consumption

but I'll take this morsel of kindness,

this exchange of kindred spirits.

I know she sees the grief I hide behind dark glasses,

but she no more mentions this than I the demons of

    oppression

that haunt her dreams and fill these long, dark days.

We know love will have to be enough for now.

Yay Bombs!

In my ears Joni sings

PEACE!

while a fighter jet passes
and social media erupts
with news of Raytheon stocks rising

ERECT!

but hardened hearts are not so enthused
nor easily seduced by the economic

BOOM!

This is no war cry on my cheek,
but sympathy for a race so very lost.[9]

No. NF-007, Australia, 1943

Epitaph for a Dove

Were you just resting

or had you given up?

Sacrificed too much,

lost your lover in the storm?

What meter of suffering

beat in your heart?

When was enough enough   for you?

I turned around to save you,

bide your time,

but my neighbor was in a hurry,

knocked you flightless to the curb,

before I could set us free.

No. 025-0715 - Sports Authority Parking
Lot, Connecticut; July 2015

Driving to Bridgeport

This is no
hand-race down
plastic tracks
with gleeful
CRAShhhhh!

Do you forget
the consequence
of flesh and bone
against external force?

I can tell you how it ends —
ashes to ashes,
dust to dust
swept to the side of the road.

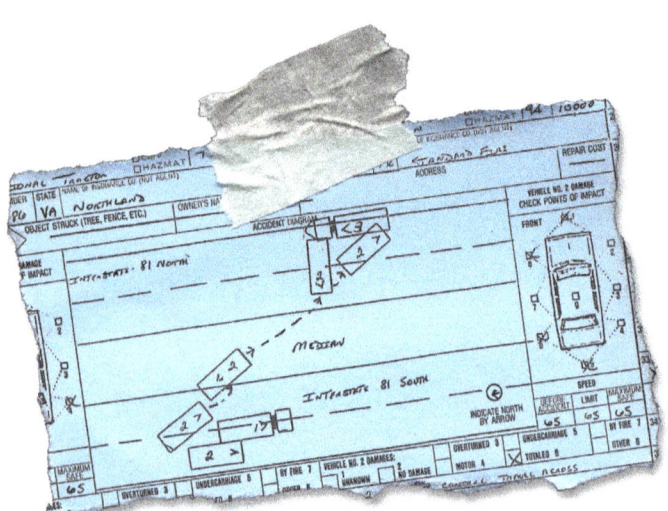

Now Trending >

A sidebar photo
leaves little
for the mind's eye.
A familiar report.
Heartbreak by hyperlink:
Interstate 81, 1 Killed.

Random news
delivered 600 miles north
on the pulse of technology
leaves me breathless
and full of memory.
If it were yesterday,
would I (click here)?
View Slideshow for details?
Find out what remains of the father, the son?

Seduced by the lure of
More Information,
how immune have we become?
Numbed and dumbed
by these machines,
we could watch you die,
then Comment Here your epitaph.

Mallard Duck (Anas platyrhynchos)

This Sad Dominion

There are bones along the tracks.
Bones bleached white
in the commuter-day sun.

Leg bones mostly,
a spine near Rowayton.
A skull or decimated baseball —
I suppose it doesn't really matter.
Not at this speed.
Not from up here.
Not if you never notice.

But how do you miss the dead duck,
her head curled against the
warm steel track in Darien?

I rub my fingers along a smooth jawbone
left in my pocket from last week's hike —
possum perhaps, raccoon?
My fingers touch its teeth like rosary beads,
penance for our collective apathy.[10]

CONTACT

Violet family (Violaceae)

"In Wildness is the preservation of the world. - Henry David Thoreau"

Central Park Morning

Sun through spring trees
feels like home —
the smell of damp woods
and morning lingering
in granite crevices.
Even Hawk
who soars above
suggests
I am Alice returned
and resting beneath
familiar branches.
Then!
Sounds of sirens
and subterfuge,
the low rumble of
a mass awakening.
As Hawk ascends to
cement parapet,
I see I am somewhere
quite removed.

No. 027-0815 - Park Trailhead,
Connecticut; August 2015

Brief Morning

Oh brief morning that bursts with beauty
   we no longer deserve.

We'll turn our heads to other things important.

As if you are eternal. As if we are.

Then gray, gray, gray out to the edge of nothing.

So Begins the Day

the 4am

Sanskrit chant

has nothing

on the bird chorus

that begins

two hours

into my day

(the sun is silent)

cat fed,

preened,

and napping now

sounds of:

coffee,

laundry,

machines that ding & buzz & chime   winding, winding,

winding   morning shift   sounds the start   the race![12]

034-0915 - Municipal Parking Lot,
Damariscotta, Maine; September 2015

As She Behaves, So Will She Be

I'll be honest,

as I saved the spider

from sure destruction

and placed him gently

on the morning sill,

I wondered

if perhaps I'd earned

a bit of karma,

if maybe the gesture

would spare me

the sure destruction

of betrayals —

disappointments.

But everyday humans

don't abide by karma,

never mind what gurus say,

so the spider went about his

and I my business for the day

knowing this:

salvation, like love, is random.

No. 039-1115 - Fall Flossing, Town Green, Connecticut; November 2015

Fate Sealed

what are those?

interrupts a stranger

in the quiet of October dunes,

watching seals bob and weave

his salt and pepper smile,

those sharp green eyes

invade my solitude   still

are they dangerous?

not as much as the sharks

i'm thinking of going for a swim, join me?

i watch as he peels off layers hiding

smooth   dark   skin

will you meet me for dinner?

he calls, diving into hungry waves

just desserts

Dangerous Ground

Trusting Faithful,

we walk across

the backs of monsters,

fire-breathing,

sulfur-churning beasts —

smiling for the camera,

licking sweets,

our tongues wagging,

when at any moment

the whole earth could shift,

send unexpected flames

that char any hope we have

of seeing the valley where,

they tell me,

the wolves mate for life.

Ekphrastic Rabbit: An Out of Body Experience

Some might see the artist's intention.
Cold War Germany via taxidermy.
The rest is explained shorthand in chalk
there beneath my stuffed and stiffened body,
something about the *temperature* and *Eurasia*.
It's difficult for me to see from my vantage point, really,
but better to face forward in perpetuity
than look back with regret on the moment
I paused just long enough to be considered now
the symbolic representation of the ability
    to span long distances.
If I were the artist, naked and tied to these
painted poles with fat and felt,
his dick as stiff as my ears,
I'd surely get more than a cursory glance,
a squeamish ewwww from the schoolgirl
still wet from the nude across the gallery.

No. 040-1115 - Flosser with Gum, Parking Lot, Connecticut; November 2015

Act of Contrition

We knew the time would come

me down here cowering

you up there towering

while the winds of change

howled at us ferociously.

We knew the time had come

me down here cowering

you up there towering

in the dawn of your last day —

before the ropes and cutters.

And when the time had come

me down here towering

you up there cowering

I took to the woods

to apologize to your brethren.

No. 045-1215 - Grocery Store Parking Lot, Christmas Eve, Connecticut; December 2015

Bury Me in Yellow

Talk about elephant in the room —
we're all dying.
You and me
and the little lost soul
we pulled from the crawl space
on Easter Sunday — *Risen!*

Despite her nine lives, she will die.
She will die.
And you will die.
And I will die.

We talk about the peripheries,
whisper the horrors of loss
as anecdotes now —
the deathbed promise,
the final breath,
the oddity of coffins.

But that sweet and painful
smell of lilies will linger
on you and on me into eternity.

The cat is spared such indignity, you say,
never to be mourned on silken pillows
in Sunday's yellow finest.

Oh tell me we can laugh this way until the end, love,
I could not bear it any other way.

No. 043-1215 - Business Park,
Connecticut; December 2015

Time Peace

This watch around my neck doesn't work.
It stopped too many years ago to count.
But I found it in a box tangled with other time-keepers
and liked the silver charms and glass beads enough to
    ignore the dead weight of its time.

I have no use for metered time —
those requisite hours defined by
mechanisms of Must and Should and Have To.
Their impetus proves too demanding, too constricting,
    wholly uninspiring.

It is not for everyone.
The lovers who've shared my bed are disturbed
    by my nightstand clock now three hours too fast.
To counterbalance, they set down weighted wristwatches
that tic-t-tic-t-tic into the night while they sleep and I
    wonder...why?

Women never seem to mind that the clock by the sofa   in
    the kitchen   above the desk
is too fast   too slow   doesn't work at all.
How easily *we* move in space with no time.

There are moments I glance at a phantom watch
    to confirm I am in-tune with some unseen schedule.
Most days, I sense the passing hours by the warmth of
    the sun, the shadows across my path, the waning
    energy of my spirit.

No. 046-0116 - Trolley Trail, Connecticut; January 2016

Flirting with Echoes

Am I flirting with echoes?

Like this Junco who skips

from branch to branch

calling to itself

in winter woods —

am I in similar pursuit?

These dreams,

these expectations

only an echo of

my imagination?

Coquette displaced

in a frozen marsh,

too early for spring?

Too lost for hope?[13]

CAPE COD SERIES

No. NF-013, Cape Cod National Seashore, 2015

Saved
Resigned,
set still
and unmoved
at the wayside.
Wings folded,
head bowed —
her endless prayer
in wait for
the viaticum...
then sudden breath
set feathers to flutter
once more.

Flotsam
I see
what is
washed up
by the sea,
what rises
to the top,
floats
to the surface
of thoughts
as feet
sink into
centuries
of refuse,
churned,
pitched,
tossed,
until they
settle,
quiet
on the
shore.

Jetsam

Someday,
someone will
find us here,
see how
we were
by the sea,
tread into
footprints
long left behind,
put our ghosts
in a pocket,
hear our
whispers
in hallways
of shells.

The Organization of Stones

The organization
of stones
is futile pursuit
here on this vast
primordial
plane.
We want to see
straight lines,
patterns,
purpose,
reason.
Yet there is
freedom in the
random,
relief when
a neat row of
stones suddenly
washes away;
so I will go,
and you will go.
Listen closely —
it's the sound
of endless
heartbeats.

Spring Beauty (Claytonia virginica)

After a long winter, the pale-rose flowers in early spring are food for the soul. - Euell Gibbons[14]

Consolations

My fingers hold tight

to winter still,

wanting the cold quiet

for tranquil pursuits,

the solitary walks

with words and wishes.

But this spring cacophony

calls loudly

disrupting poems!

and startling prayers!

Such demands.

Such demands.

Oh, but those sweet

ephemeral wonders,

they do offer small

and hopeful

consolation I suppose.

Pagan Prayer for a Friend

In the east this night
great hunter rises,
masked in bared trees
and mists of heaven.
The triad heralds
his arrival.

Today, we saw
stone titans,
erratics drawn by glacier.
Triad too, aligned
along our path,
in ancient woods —
by God's hand
or mechanism of man?

Stolen time for us,
this winter walk.
Spoken word and
friendship's pace
come easily now,
but time is precious
as life and blood bear down
on her with ties that bind
too tightly to breathe.

The One in whose image
she was made asked Job
"Can you loosen Orion's belt?"[15]
on premise that He could.
Can she not, then?

Oh glorious
Alnitak! Alnilam! Mintaka!
Show her light
and give strength
that she may
find breath and
reach for the stars!

The names of the three stars in Orion's belt: Alnitak, Alnilam, Mintaka.

Resistance is Futile

How easily I write

of changing seasons,

life grown from death.

Circle of Life,

I pontificate

with heels dug firm.

But at Sunday service

in wooded cathedral

as summer genuflects,

and jewel weed with wild grapes

stand at the crossing...

Everything is flowing,

god whispers.

How foolish am I to resist?

No. 047-0216 - Behind Armored Vehicle, Connecticut; February 2016

Epiphany

Before sleep had left bones

with dreams still whispering,

as fleeting as the sunrise,

for one short ray of understanding.

Without need for scripture or sacrifice,

tithe, temple or testament.

No spokesperson or man behind a curtain

pulling levers of smoke and smite.

Not all-knowing, all-powerful,

no rules and regulations in 6-point type.

Just you and me and our daily bread:

how we love one another.

 An ouroboros is a circular symbol depicting a snake eating its tail used as an emblem of wholeness or infinity.

Prima Materia

The snake when it sheds its skin surely must pause,
writhe in curiosity at leaving part of itself behind,
wonder at the scars and marks of time,
consider for a moment its perverted trail,
the bending, winding path of ending
the bending, winding path of becoming.

Am I the ouroboros?

The alpha and omega?

Or am I nothing at all?
Soon to be your ashes,
the dust and duff of the forest,
the peat of your mythology
and the lies you tell yourself.[16]

No. 051-0216 - Shopping Plaza, Connecticut; February 2016

Sanctified without Assistance

This is sacred space.
It needs no adornment,
sanctified without assistance.

In the spring
sweet green rejoices,
sings hallelujah at the unfurl.

Then summer's
broad leaf and life —
a grand chorus from hallowed woods.

In fall,
the bright colors
play a crescendoed reminder:

*To everything there is a season,
And a time to every purpose under heaven.*[17]

Come winter,
bare-branch whispers
of hope promised, stored.

This is sacred space
without adornment,
adulation ever on.

CONNECTION

At night I went out into the dark and saw a glimmering star and heard a frog, and Nature seemed to say, Well do not these suffice?
– Ralph Waldo Emerson[18]

Green Frog (Rana clamitans)

And They Will Have Eden at Last

It will be the frog

that heralds His arrival

with the great singsong

of the forest primeval,

and all its brethren

will rejoice

that final judgement,

the great exodus

of righteous and sinful,

reclaim the very

foundation of the world

with a deafening, holy chorus.

No. 053-0216 - Valentine's Day, Italian Bistro, Connecticut; February 2016

Tempest

The trees lament

the menacing storm.

Their haunted cries

travel on the wind,

force entry

through rafters

and walls.

Smells of memory

resurrected...

on a day

that begins with

a crack in the sky.

No. 050-0216 - Snow Bank, Connecticut; February 2016

Benevolence

Righteous one, dear Chickadee,

she'll drop every tenth seed or so,

as dawn illuminates her black velvet cap,

snow blows against a feather-white scarf.

At once, Sunday's song begins

and the choir takes to its seats

perched on high above the sacred feast.

Blessed for these small portals of kindness,

she is generous in her meter,

the Sparrows grateful for the tithe.

No. 055-0316 – "Beautiful," Daycare Parking Lot, Connecticut; March 2016

So soon?

I do love the surprise of sudden bloom,

though not as much as winter's calm,

    its luxury of quiet.

Can't we have a few more days?

Or is this spring come so soon?

No. 056-0316 - Winter Field,
Connecticut; March 2016

El Niño

They speak your name

as if you are a Spanish lover,

exotic and mysterious,

with attention to the curve of your accent.

But there is no mystery

to your inclinations,

you are no stranger to me —

neither winsome nor welcome.

You have stolen fire from my hearth

and quiet from still and silent days;

my lover lost to the bed's cool side,

while I'm left with birdsong in winter.

Let them fall into your warm embrace,

but I know your fair-weather nature.

No. 054-0316- Post Office,
Connecticut; March 2016

First!

vernal pool
appears!

pond peepers
sing!

muddy dog
runs!

butterfly
lifts off!

osprey
soars!

spring
begins!

Mourning Cloak

She is the surest sign

of spring, that one.

She with her cloak

of burgundy brown.

The palest rays of sun

that kiss its hem,

her blue eyes belie,

no hint of despair or grief.

But curiosity!

And sweet relief!

Mourning Cloak (Nymphalis antiopa)

Beacon Hill on Sunday

Mourning Cloak escort

through spring woods finds

Jays on high alert and

a pair of Wild Turkeys

in vocal discourse.

No less than eight

Ospreys swoop and swirl,

with no regrets.

Just one Egret.

Two Vireo,

in stereo,

chartreuse!

No. 059-0516 - Intermediate School, Connecticut; May 2016

Morning Solo
For Mary

The one bird at 5:53 tells me morning is on its way.

My friend Mary would remind me of the chorus soon to follow, how bird by bird they witness our ever turning, ever spinning.

I never noticed the crescendo before her note pinned to a page, the observation of a poet revealing how the world sings ever on.

No. 060-0516 - Walmart, Connecticut; May 2016

Chanting

Without the luxury

of love,

lone willet

calls into the fog

and I respond,

as if our one and one

make two.

A mystic algebra,

always searching

for the missing,

lone willet

calls into the fog

and I respond.

In Spring Woods, Maple

It is your tell-tale heart —

the red that beats

so softly

to the rhythm

of the breeze.

In the stillness

I hear its cadence,

feel its pulse

beneath my feet.

Life renewed

against blue sky.

April Snow

It's as if she'd forgotten something,

traveled half-way down the street

then turned around with a high-winded sigh,

upended a box marked "Needs Refrigeration"

   on the front lawn,

blew a cold kiss with a wicked grin and left again,

her final *ta-ta* the bitter breeze.

No. 061-0616 - Terrarium at the Ob/Gyn,
Connecticut; June 2016

Evidence of Fairies

There is a path I walk along

that seems of ancient time.

Low-bent branches

and carpets of moss.

A convocation of

creatures and spirits

who move about

with rustle of leaves

and cryptic speech.

A corduroy road, then

makeshift footbridges

cross giggling streams,

and walking sticks

prop themselves against

century-old trees as if

a visitor sits where I cannot see.

And every now and then,

I am certain I find

evidence of fairies.

An Odd Courting

(A 100-Word True Story)

I assure you, I did nothing to encourage him. I was simply kneeling trailside, counting petals on a flower — *he loves me, he loves me not, he loves me, he loves me not.*

Then I heard him approach, footstepping through memories of trees scattered across the forest floor. In his camouflage, I recognized fear and wonder, the wild and unpredictable nature of things, the magic of connection.

There was no amorous announcement to *my* ear, but a sound, a something sound I could not believe. So as not to dash any hopes, I left quietly, wondering: do spiders really sing?

Male Wolf Spiders create a love song for nearby female spiders by causing leaves to vibrate and sending out an auditory song.[19]

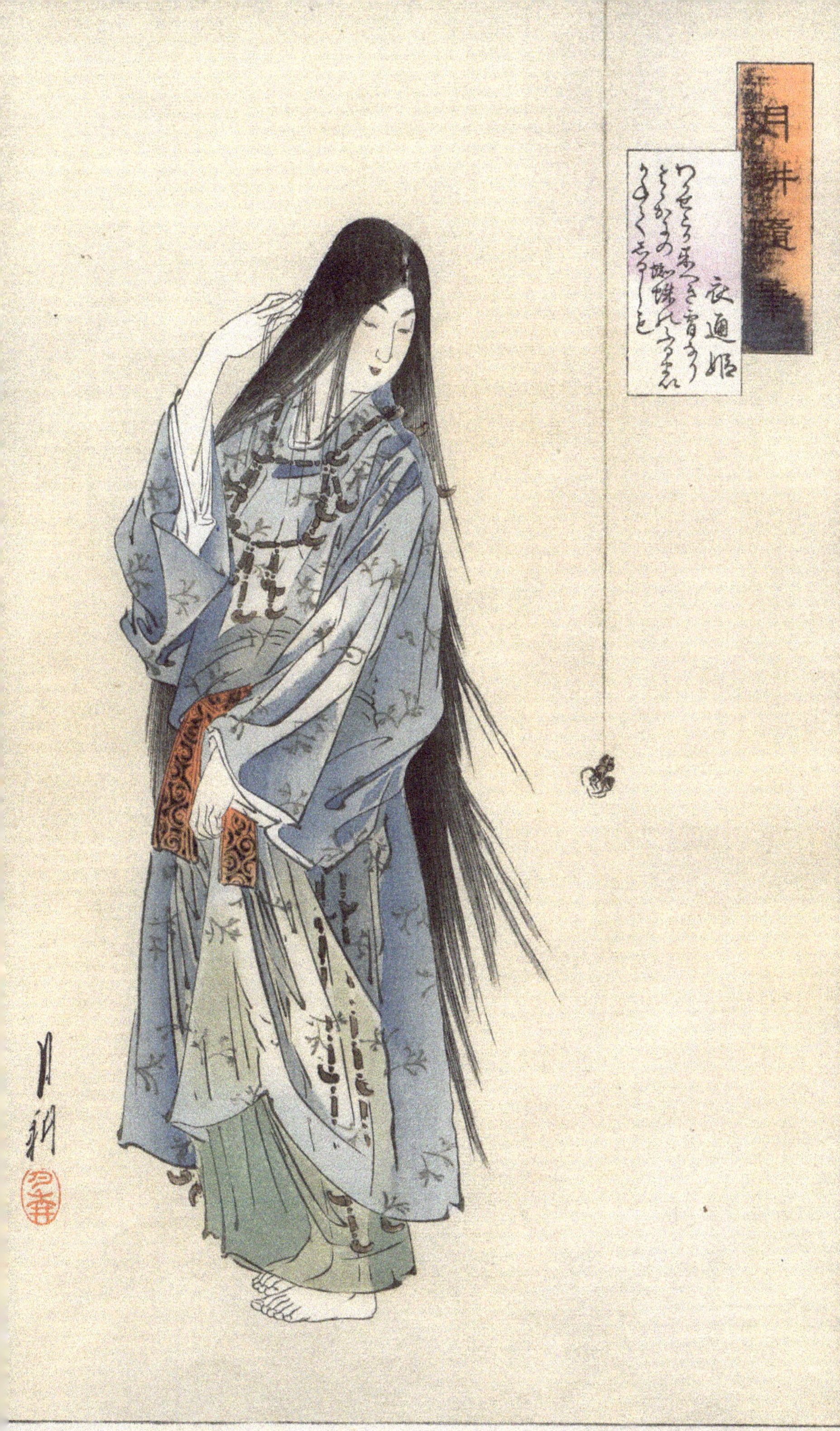

月耕随筆
衣通姫
わかせこか来へき宵なり
さゝかにの蜘蛛のふるまひ
かねてしるしも
月耕

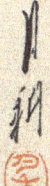

Microcosm

The spider had a curious look —

not curious as in odd,

but curious, inquisitive, intrigued.

I saw him from the corner of my eye

watching me,

then rummaging

through a pile of paper,

back again for a second look,

peering as if to say *Who Are YOU?*

(or WHAT I suppose)

Perhaps the same look of WHAT?

the fish had as it soared over the pond

yesterday afternoon...

Who are YOU? to the osprey,

and *WHEN did I learn to fly?*

No. 062-0616 - Flosser with Paperclip at the ATM, Connecticut; June 2016

No. 064-0616 - Flosser and Bone, Connecticut Parking Lot; June 2016

No. 065-0716 - Birthday Flosser,
Rest Area, Massachusetts; July 2016

Meditation on a Weekday Walk

In this my new occupation

I will preach from the pulpit,

soar reconnaissance with the pileated,

nursemaid a wood duck's brood,

survey the marsh with an egret,

meditate with the painted turtles

on a rock or the pine felled in a storm,

no matter, my profit immeasurable.

Spotted turtle (Clemmys guttata)

In tales told by many Native Americans, the World Turtle carries the earth upon its back.[20]

I Am Just the World

Pay no attention.

I'm just here

beneath these trees,

their forgotten leaves

warm from the sun.

Never mind

my slow traverse,

I'll step aside for you.

Make myself small

so you forget

I am light and love,

the god to which you pray,

the universe upon my back,

everything.

No. 068-0716 - Post Office, Connecticut; July 2016

Sustenance

The gull tosses

the crab

with as much

JOY

as the osprey

overhead

displays

his catch

and I

breathe

the fresh

sea air.

The Rocks at Nauset Beach

I would make them my diadem

string a row on golden twine
to wear around my neck

place the smallest in a cradle
set upon a finger, here

wrap them round my wrist
to keep tide's time   and mine

Green

Surely the palette
with which She chose
to paint this day
was called Spring Rain
and every shade
of green ended with an !

Tree Spirit Parting

She told me she was leaving

long before either of us knew.

Each day for weeks

she called out as I passed —

whispering secrets

and ancient stories

into the wind.

I heard her — sweet Maple —

casting memories out

on the breath of family.

And then she was no more.

That same breath

in which she took part

for thousands of days

brought her down   to start again.

A year before the fall.
Sugar Maple (Acer saccharum)

Daisy Fleabane (Erigeron annuus)

Summer Whisper

Yesterday, while I stood

knee-deep in meadow grass

to capture wild fleabane

and raspberries in bloom,

as a joyful bee dipped

and danced in front of me,

I almost missed the visitor

who flew quickly down the path.

I think she thought I was

a flower — leftover perfumes from the day —

but stopped just shy of my pistil

when she realized I was not.

It took a while to focus,

I felt her before I saw,

so close was she

I felt the breeze

of her magic little wings.

"Summer's coming,"

the hummingbird whispered,

then she floated off to

honeysuckle waiting

just nearby.

Great Spangled Fritillary
(Speyeria cybele)

Carpe Diem

From the window:

a butterfly

orange and playful

floats across

the hot green backdrop

of summer.

Like wings,

my thoughts flutter

here, there,

alight on

unpredictable life

as catbird

scans, soars,

seize the day

sweet arrhythmia

gone!

No. 069-0816 - Car Rental Office, Connecticut; August 2016

SUMMER TOP TEN

1. Colors

zinnia
dahlia
dianthus
coreopsis
liatris
cosmos
delphinium
geranium
hydrangea
fresia
gladiolus
mari-gold

2. Feet

bare feet
on hot pavement
with colorful painted toes
flip flops
hiding in sand

3. Secrets

summer places
 — like Brigadoon from the mists —
a screen porch for lazy afternoons
a food truck serving lobster
a picnic-table feast in a clearing of trees,
a secret garden of flowers and bees

4. Flavors

watermelon
raspberry, blueberry, strawberry
snap peas
corn-on-the-cob (more butter please)
cucumber
zucchini
basil and thyme
(have you got the time?)
oregano
tomato
string bean
peach, plum
nectarine

5. Critters

never mind the spider
who lives outside my window
or the bugs that accompany my walks
say hello to
dragon flies and butterflies
I always do
to frogs and turtles
to chipmunks in scurry
and birds in trees

6. Scenic Views

you forget in winter
what the bare bones look like
bedecked in robes of green
and veils of robin-egg blue,
how the heat of summer
lingers in whispers
on the horizon
and in the reflections
at the end of days

7. Sounds

cicada
cricket
peepers
thunder
fireworks
motorcycle
tell me it is summer still

8. Vacation

tepid morning
tossing suitcases in back seat
and cooler with treats
on the road
Simon and Garfunkel
(or just Simon sometimes)
windows down
windows up
noon
sandwiches from plastic bags
are we there yet?
sound of tires on gravel
in a parking lot
somewhere else

9. Memories

She kept filet mignon
in a freezer by the door,
back-to-back
with the grill outside.
We'd pick giant red tomatoes
along her fence out back
then drive 45 minutes up the road
for fresh corn-on-the cob.
A gallon of iced tea
mixed with lemonade
sloshed in the Tupperware pitcher
I remember from when I was four.
We sat out on the patio
— ancient umbrellas
shading us from afternoon sun —
and watched bees get drunk
on corn butter and Dad's beer.

10. Enjoyment

There is always someone
somewhere
enjoying this day
at the beach around the corner
in the yard next door
along the trail in the woods
and the park across town —
little kids
and big kids
and dogs
can I play too?

THE ALICE POEMS

No. 071-0916 - Mousehouse Cheesehaus, Wisconsin; September 2016

Dear Alice...

Oh Alice.

There are some who would call us lewd,
my kindred, for our admiration
of these domed sentinels,
our arduous prostration
somehow deviant (or provocative).

Oh Alice.

Still others will point to
dear Lewis' penchant for
their psychotropic disposition
as reason for your very existence,
and for my own fascination here, too.

Oh Alice.

If they only knew our true motivation,
why we take to bended knee.
That it be not sex or drugs,
but these harbingers of rich fertility
that rock with creativity,
and roll our imaginations.

No. 072-0916 - Badlands National Park,
South Dakota; September 2016

Mushroom in a Pot

Who is the interloper
greeting me this morning?
Did I leave the door open?
A window, perhaps?
Is that how you arrived,
took up residence
with Violet,
demanded smile
and surprise
before the sun?
I do hope you'll
stay awhile,
share these
first few rays of
Wednesday
and news of Alice.

No. 073-0916 - Badlands National Park,
South Dakota; September 2016

Forest Fellow
(A 100-Word True Story)

I saw a stranger bent over, studying the base of a tree just up the path.

"What are you looking at?" I asked, feeling curiouser and curiouser.

"Mushrooms," he told me, "these." Then he bowed and plucked a bouquet from the log at my feet. "Edible," he explained with a smile.

"What are you making?" I asked, and he replied, "Oyster mushrooms with a sherry cream sauce."

Mouths watering, we talked a bit about wild woods and food fare before parting ways.

"Dear, dear," I thought, "I forgot to ask *Who are you?* How will I ever find him again?"

Ode to Fungi

On bended knee
I bow to your

creativity

fertility

singularity

your

simplicity

and dignity

...absurdity?

Divinity.

No. 074-0916 - Spearfish Canyon, South Dakota; September 2016

A Knowing Way
For Matt

He is of water born,
bred with the taste of
salt on his tongue
and sea air in his lungs.

He knows the
change of season,
the approaching storm,
the moment the water
will shimmer like glass.

The tide glides
through his veins,
in and out of a heart
that loves the water,
loves the shoreline
embracing
this primordial brew.

Found landbound,
he calls the trees by name,
speaks to birds of prey
both kin and ken,
in great companionship;
the sky his breath,
the woods and marsh
his hallowed refuge.

To transform the world, we must begin with ourselves... - J. Krishnamurti[21]

Bird Removed

i am bird
removed

sky
breath

sun
crown

feather
dress

song
my solitary
intent

shared
heaven

spared
god

i fly
free

MISC.

No. 007-1214 - Diner,
Connecticut; December 2014

INDEX OF POEMS

A Knowing Way 139
A Lament for the Parcel at 250 North Main Street 4
A New York City Schooling 29
A Righteous Man Regardeth the Life of His Beast 27
Act of Contrition 57
An Odd Courting 105
And They Will Have Eden at Last 83
April Snow 101
As She Behaves, So Will She Be 49
Beacon Hill on Sunday 95
Benevolence 87
Bird Removed 141
Brief Morning 45
Bury Me in Yellow 59
Cape Cod Series 65
Carpe Diem 121
Central Park Morning 43
Chanting 99
Common Ground Series 29
Consolations 69
Dangerous Ground 53
Dear Alice 131
Driving to Bridgeport 36
Ekphrastic Rabbit: An Out of Body Experience 54
El Niño 91
Epiphany 75
Epitaph for a Dove 34
Evidence of Fairies 103
Evidence of Flossing: A Random Riff 8
False Hope 30
Fate Sealed 51
First! 93
Flirting with Echoes 63
Flotsam 66
Forest Fellow 135
Green 116
Grocery Store: November 2016 31

I Am Just the World	111
In Spring Woods, Maple	100
Jetsam	67
Losing My Religion	19
Mass, Shooting, God, Guns	17
Meditation on a Weekday Walk	109
Microcosm	107
Morning Solo	97
Mountain Breeze™	7
Mourning Cloak	94
Mushroom in a Pot	133
Now Trending >	37
Nuisance Species	24
Ode to Fungi	137
Pagan Prayer for a Friend	70
Prima Materia	77
Project Limulus	22
Resistance is Futile	73
Sanctified without Assistance	79
Saved	66
Sixth Day	21
So Begins the Day	46
So soon?	89
Summer Top Ten	123
Summer Whisper	119
Sunday at the Dollar Store	15
Sustenance	113
Tempest	85
The Alice Poems	129
The Grand Intention	xix
The Organization of Stones	67
The Promise of More	13
The Rocks at Nauset Beach	115
The Times They Are a Changin'	3
They Know Not What They Do	11
This Sad Dominion	39
Time Peace	61
Tree Spirit Parting	117
Yay Bombs!	32

No. 077-0914- Yellowstone National
Park, Wyoming; September 2016

ENDNOTES

You'll notice several references to Lewis Carroll's *Alice in Wonderland* throughout this book. She is my kindred spirit, I suppose. But then again, who doesn't feel like Alice sometimes — a little lost, a little curious, filled with wonder, yet wondering "which way I ought to go from here?"

Here are some other notes of interest and acknowledgement...

About the POEMS

The poems in the Common Ground Series ("A New York Schooling," "False Hope," and "Grocery Store: November 2016") were written during the 2016 U.S. presidential campaign. They first appeared together in *Inauguration Nation*, an exhibit at Kehler Liddell Gallery in New Haven, Connecticut (January 2017), curated by Tom Edwards and Tracey Scheer. See www.kehlerliddellgallery.com.

The poem "Tempest" was originally published in *The Aurorean*, Fall/Winter 2013-2014.

The poems "Evidence of Faeries," "Ode to Fungi," and "Summer Whisper" originally appeared in the book *LOOK UP! Musings on the Nature of Mindfulness* (2014), but asked to be included in this one, too.

About the REFERENCES

1. Here is more of the John Muir quote as it appears in *My First Summer in the Sierra* (Boston and New York: Houghton Mifflin, 1911), p. 211: "When we try to pick out anything by itself, we find it hitched to everything else in the universe. One fancies a heart like our own must be beating in every crystal and cell, and we feel like stopping to speak to the plants and animals as friendly fellow-mountaineers. Nature as a poet, an enthusiastic workingman, becomes more and more visible the farther and higher we go...."

2. Isaac Newton's Third Law of Motion.

3. Matthew 25:40, paraphrased.

4. Muir, *My First Summer in the Sierra*, p. 211.

5. Head, Tom, ed. *Conversations with Carl Sagan*, (Jackson, MS: University Press of Mississippi, 2006), p. 62.

6   The poem lists the actual ingredients in Purex "Mountain Breeze"™ laundry detergent.

7   The title of the poem refers to the sixth day of creation, as explained in the Bible, Genesis 1:24-25: "And God said, Let the earth bring forth the living creatures after his kind, cattle, and creeping things, and beasts of the earth after his kind: and it was so. And God made the beasts of the earth after his kind, and cattle after their kind, and every thing that creepeth upon the earth after his kind: and God saw that *it was* good."

8   Statistics and notes about the English Starling can be attributed as follows: (a) world population figure from February 2017, Worldometers.info; (b) "The Last Place on Earth without Human Noise," by Rachel Nuwer, BBC, January 2014 (https://tinyurl.com/lj6ysbm); (c) common cold statistic, National Institute of Allergy and Infectious Diseases; Center for Disease Control, February 2017; (d) effects of DRC-1339, Thomas J. Decino, Donald J. Cunningham and Edward W. Schafer, *The Journal of Wildlife Management*, Vol. 30, No. 2 (Apr., 1966); (e) "Dead birds dropping from a tree in West Springfield causes community unrest," WGGB/WSHM, January 2017 (https://tinyurl.com/y7ylk2hr); and (f) "Starlings," A Passion for Nature website, Jennifer Schlick, (https://tinyurl.com/y6wzl5uf).

9   A nod to the song *California* by Joni Mitchell, 1970.

10 Title comes from the Bible reference in Genesis 1:26: "Let us make man in our image, after our likeness. And let them have dominion over the fish of the sea, and over the birds of the heavens and over the livestock and over all the earth and over every creeping thing that creeps on the earth."

11 The quote is from Henry David Thoreau's essay "Walking." *Atlantic Monthly*, vol. 9 (1862), as found on Project Guttenberg, revised November 2010, http://www.gutenberg.org (http://goo.gl/FHeg).

12   Written with gratitude to Krishna Das for "4AM Hanuman Chalisa," from the album *Kirtan Wallah*, 2014.

13   While a junco is a common winter sighting in Connecticut, the coquette is a hummingbird found in Central and South American. Read the double entendre as you will, of course — bird, flirt, floozy.

14   This quote is from Euell Gibbons' *Stalking the Wild Asparagus* (New York: David McKay Co., 1970), p. 203.

15   As referenced in the Bible, Job 38:31, in which God challenges Job: "Can you bind the chains of the Pleiades? Can you loosen Orion's belt? Can you bring forth the constellations in their seasons or lead out the Bear with its cubs? Do you know the laws of the heavens? Can you set up God's dominion over the earth?"

16   The title refers to prima materia, a formless primeval substance regarded as the original material of the universe.

17   With reference to the Bible passage in Ecclesiastes 3: 1-8: "To every thing there is a season, and a time to every purpose under the heaven: a time to be born, and a time to die; a time to plant, and a time to pluck up that which is planted; a time to kill, and a time to heal; a time to break down, and a time to build up; a time to weep, and a time to laugh; a time to mourn, and a time to dance; a time to cast away stones, and a time to gather stones together; a time to embrace, and a time to refrain from embracing; a time to get, and a time to lose; a time to keep, and a time to cast away; a time to rend, and a time to sew; a time to keep silence, and a time to speak; a time to love, and a time to hate; a time of war, and a time of peace." (But I always hear it as the Simon and Garfunkel song.)

18   This is a quote by Ralph Waldo Emerson, from *The Heart of Emerson's Journals*. Ed. Bliss Perry. (Boston: Houghton Mifflin, 1926), p. 127.

19 My ah-ha moment came from "Listen to The Creepy Sounds Spiders Make When They Want Sex," by Ed Mazza, *Huffington Post*, May 26, 2015. (This link includes two audio clips so you can hear a spider sing, too: https://tinyurl.com/m9227z2.)

20 Quote about the World Turtle by Lorena Stookey from the *Thematic Guide to World Mythology* (Westport, CT: Greenwood Press, 2004), p. 15.

21 "To transform the world, we must begin with ourselves; and what is important in beginning with ourselves is the intention. The intention must be to understand ourselves and not to leave it to others to transform themselves or to bring about a modified change through revolution, either of the left or of the right." Quote by J. Krishnamurti, from *The First and Last Freedom* (Harper & Row, 1975), chapter 4. As seen on www.jkrishnamurti.org, June 2017. Please read more: https://tinyurl.com/y7ba8m2j.

About the IMAGES

Cover/Introduction - Credit: Hubble/ESA (European Space Agency)/NASA. Reproduced with permission. This globular cluster of stars known as Palomar 12 was imaged by Hubble's Advanced Camera for Surveys. When describing this image on www.nasa.gov, NASA writer Karl Hille writes about Panta Rhei, "a simplified version of the famous Greek philosopher Heraclitus' teachings. It basically means, everything flows. And everything in the Universe is indeed continually on the move, spiraling and shifting through space."

Dental Flosser Patent Illustrations - Courtesy of Google Patents. Inventor Auguste Baumeister, patent granted January 21, 1902.

"The Grand Intention" - Keep America Beautiful, ad campaign poster, Iron Eyes Cody (a.k.a. the Crying Indian), ca. early-1970, Courtesy: CSU Archives /Everett Collection, Inc./Alamy.

"A Lament for the Parcel at 250 North Main Street" - Before photo, Map Data ©2015, Google; after photo, Map Data ©2017, Google.

"Construct of Fools" - Photo by Kevin Macaranas Domantay; Castaic, CA. Reproduced with permission.

"Project Limulus" - Illustration from *The Sea For Sam* by W. Maxwell Reed & Wilfrid S. Bronson, Illustrated by Wilfrid S. Bronson (New York: Harcourt, Brace and Company, 1935). Photo of a Horseshoe Crab Harvest, 1928. Board of Agriculture Glass Negative Collection, Delaware Public Archives.

"Yay Bombs!" - Argus (Melbourne, Vic.) (1943). Members of the Wardens' Women's Auxiliary making for the scene of an incident. Creative Commons Attribution 3.0 Australia.

"Dangerous Ground" - Illustration from a warning sign at Yellowstone National Park, Wyoming.

"Ekphrastic Rabbit: An Out of Body Experience" - Joseph Beuys, *Eurasia Siberian Symphony 1963*, © 2017 Artists Rights Society (ARS), New York / VG Bild-Kunst, Bonn. Reprinted with permission. Photo by Jen Payne.

"Pagan Prayer for a Friend" - Orion constellation illustration from *Sidereus Nuncius* (known in English as *Starry Messenger*), written and illustrated by Galileo in 1610.

"Prima Materia" - The ouroboros illustration shows The Device of Barthélemy Aneau, A Ring Eternal and Transient, "Let this be my device: for clearly I am made of mortal body and eternal soul." From *Aneau, Barthélemy: Picta poesis* (1552). Reproduced by permission of University of Glasgow Library, Special Collections.

"Mourning Cloak" - The painted Mourning Cloak is by William Lewin, *The Papilios of Great Britain* (London: J. Johnson, 1795).

"An Odd Courting" - Princess Sotoori and Spider from the *Series Zuihitsu* (Essays) by Ogata Gekko, 1887. Image printed with permission and supplied from the Humphries Collection courtesy of Ogatagekko.net.

"I Am Just the World" - The Hindu Earth, From *Popular Science Monthly*, Volume 10, 1877.

"Bird Removed" - Vintage photo by Chippix.

About the BOOK

Fonts used in *Evidence of Flossing* include Universe, Rough Typewriter, Stampwriter-Kit, and Stamp Act. The handwritten font Morsal is used with permission (and gratitude) from Letterhend (creativemarket.com/letterhend).

About FLOSSER FINDING

It's inevitable that if you start paying attention to something, you start to see it more often. It's called the Baader-Meinhof Phenomenon, or "frequency illusion" as coined by Stanford linguistics professor Arnold Zwicky. Anyone who has followed along on this book's journey can tell you, you WILL start to see flossers. This *flosser phenomenon* can be seen on the following pages, more evidence of flossing sent to me from friends over the past three years >>

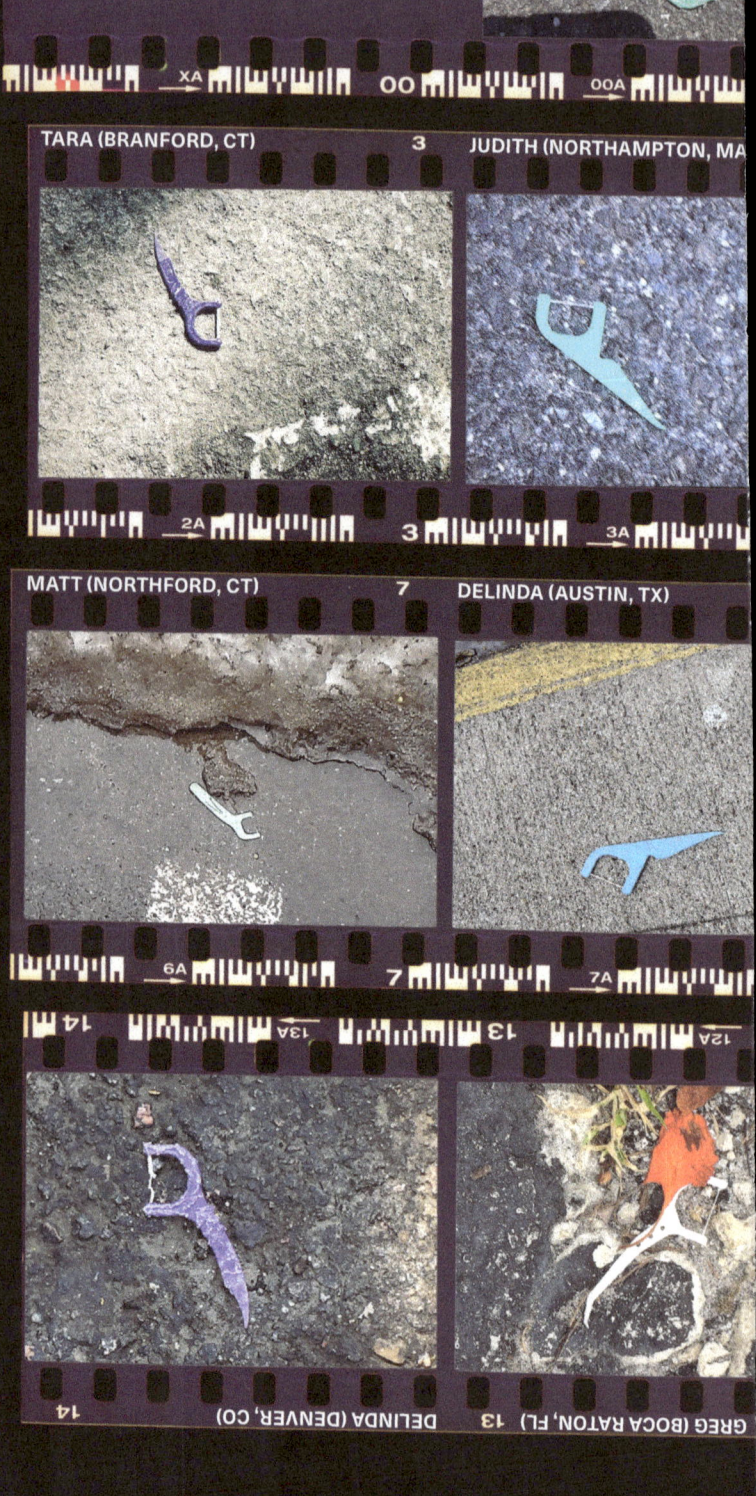

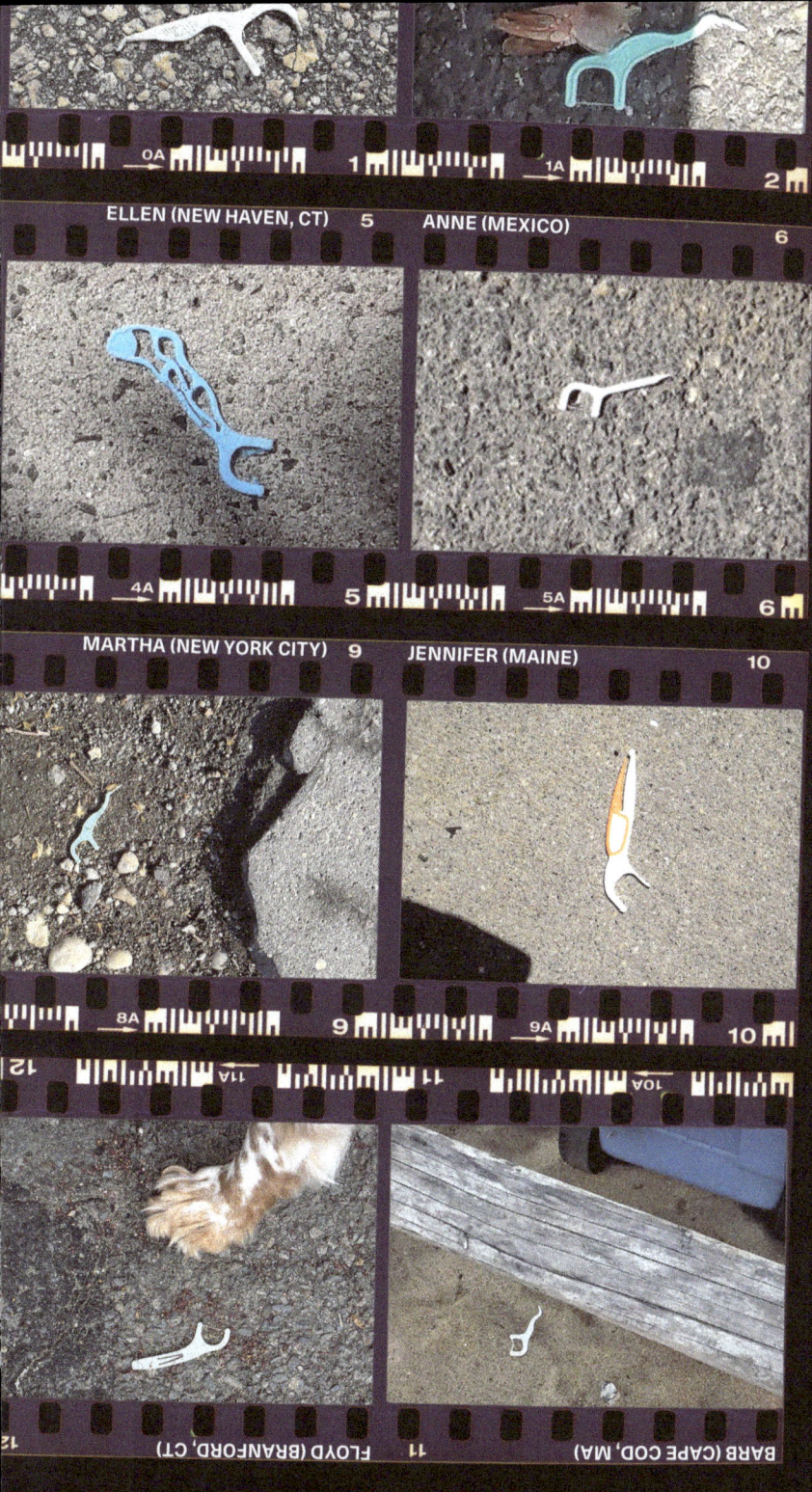

Photo by Christine Chiocchio
(Branford, CT)

ABOUT THE AUTHOR

Jen Payne is inspired by those life moments that move us most — love and loss, joy and disappointment, milestones and turning points. Her writing serves as witness to these in the form of poetry, creative non-fiction, flash fiction and essay. When she is not exploring our connections with one another, she enjoys writing about our relationships with nature, creativity, and mindfulness, and how these offer the clearest path to finding balance in our frenetic, spinning world.

Very often, her writing is accompanied by her own photography and artwork. As both a graphic designer and writer, Jen believes that partnering visuals and words layers the intentions of her work, and makes the communication more palpable.

In 2014, she published *LOOK UP! Musings on the Nature of Mindfulness*, a collection of essays, poems and original photography. *Evidence of Flossing: What We Leave Behind* is her second book.

Jen is the owner of Words by Jen, a graphic design and creative services company founded in 1993, based in Branford, Connecticut. She is a member of the Arts Council of Greater New Haven, the Connecticut Poetry Society, Guilford Arts Center, the Guilford Poets Guild, and the Independent Book Publishers Association.

Installations of her poetry were featured in *Inauguration Nation* an exhibition at Kehler Liddell Gallery in New Haven (2017), and *Shuffle & Shake* at the Arts Council of Greater New Haven (2016). Her writing has been published by *The Aurorean*, *Six Sentences*, the Story Circle Network, WOW! Women on Writing, and *The Perch*, a publication by the Yale Program for Recovery and Community Health.

You can read more of her writing on her blog *Random Acts of Writing*, www.randomactsofwriting.net.

Three Chairs Publishing

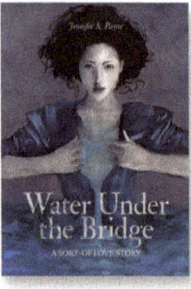

**Water Under
the Bridge**
A Sort-of Love Story
by Jennifer A. Payne
130 pgs, 5x7, $16.00

**Look Up! Musings on the
Nature of Mindfulness**
Jennifer A. Payne
288 pages, 5×7,
color photos, $25.00

**Waiting Out
the Storm**
Poetry chapbook
by Jennifer A. Payne
44 pgs, 5.5 x 8.5, $16.00

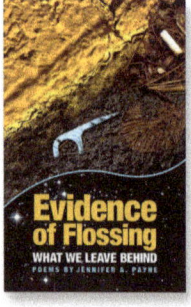

**Evidence of Flossing:
What We Leave Behind**
by Jennifer A. Payne
180 pgs, 5.5 x 8.5,
color photos, $25.00

Conversations in Print: Books, Art & More
P.O. Box 453 • Branford, CT 06405
3chairspublishing.com

www.ingramcontent.com/pod-product-compliance
Lightning Source LLC
Chambersburg PA
CBHW040328300426
44113CB00020B/2685